THE RULES OF INTERNATIONAL POLITICS

JAMES HAWK

Made with ♥ on the Notion Press Platform
www.notionpress.com

To the World Politics and States.

Contents

RULE-I: What is World?

Remember:

"WORLD IS DANGEROUS PLACE".

*"HERE YOU WILL NOT FIND **LOVERS** AND **HATERS**
BUT **TRAITORS**".*

RULE-II: Traits of International Politics

Remember:

*"ONE CAN BE REMAIN STABLE IN INTERNATIONAL POLITICS WHO HAS SHARP **SKILL** AND SHARP **SKULL**".*

RULE-III: Who is Man ?

Remember:

"A MAN IS WHO HATE DOMINATION BUT LOVE TO DOMINATE".

RULE-IV: Traits of the Great Powers-I

Remember:

"GREAT POWERS NEVER BLAME THEY SILENTLY PLAY THE GAMES IN ORDER TO ACHIEVE THEIR CLAIMS".

RULE-V: Traits of Great Powers-II

Remember:

"GREAT POWERS NEVER REST AS THEY BELIEVE IN UNREST".

RULE-VI: Traits of Great Powers-III

Remember:

*"GREAT POWERS NEVER USE THEIR **HARD POWERS** ON MINOR POWERS BECAUSE EVEN **SOFT POWERS** OF GREAT POWERS CAN DESTROY MINORS IN FEW MOVEMENT".*

RULE-VII: What is International Politics?

Remember:

"INTERNATIONAL POLITICS IS ALL ABOUT POWER EQUILIBRIUM".

RULE-VIII: About Interest

Remember:

*"IN INTERNATIONAL POLITICS, **SELF-INTEREST** ALWAYS LIES IN **MUTUAL INTEREST**".*

RULE-IX: War and Peace

Remember:

"PEACE IS POSSIBLE AFTER END OF THE WAR AND WAR IS POSSIBLE AFTER END OF THE PEACE".

RULE-X: What is State?

Remember:

"STATE IS A PLACE WHERE POLITICAL ANIMAL LIKE A MAN IS RESIDES".

www.ingramcontent.com/pod-product-compliance
Lightning Source LLC
Chambersburg PA
CBHW050819160726
48004CB00002B/921